Kieron Williamson
COMING TO LIGHT

Kieron Williamson

COMING TO LIGHT

THE REMARKABLE STORY OF A CHILD'S GIFT FOR PAINTING

As told by his parents Michelle and Keith Williamson
his mentors, teachers and friends.

First published in Great Britain in 2012

British Library Cataloguing-in-Publication Data
A CIP record for this title is available from the British Library

ISBN 978 1 906690 39 7

HALSTAR
Halsgrove House,
Ryelands Business Park,
Bagley Road, Wellington, Somerset TA21 9PZ
Tel: 01823 653777   Fax: 01823 216796
email: sales@halsgrove.com

Part of the Halsgrove group of companies
Information on all Halsgrove titles is available at: www.halsgrove.com

Printed and bound in China by Everbest Printing Co Ltd

FOREWORD
Michael Hill

I remain in a privileged and quite unique position to continue witnessing the incredible reaction to Kieron Williamson's fascinating world of art. To have found myself able to assist and encourage Kieron at the very beginning of his whirlwind journey has been a most enlightening experience. How fitting that this book should now be published to enable Kieron's extraordinary story to be told.

My personal links with Keith and Michelle Williamson span many years and I have nothing but the highest admiration for the way in which they have both managed to cope under the pressures that have surrounded the talents of their gifted son. In such a short time, the Williamson family have had to learn to balance all the demands of exciting media opportunities against the harmony, protection and normality of a home life. This balancing act has only be made possible through their dedication and unfailing love for Kieron.

Of course, Kieron simply sails along, almost oblivious to the impact that he has made – and continues to make. He remains a bright, intelligent, happy little boy, no different to any other child of his age. He is a joy to be with and a marvel to watch when he is painting. Whenever we have spent time studying pictures together I am entranced by his quick-witted observations and incredibly mature opinions on painting techniques. His knowledge has been gained through having an acute awareness of everything that surrounds him. His development of painting has been meteoric and his ability to approach, assess and subsequently capture his chosen subject in watercolour, oil or pastel is thoroughly professional at all times.

I have encountered many who try to analyse the Kieron phenomena. They question his ability, wrestle over his style and deliberate over his range of subject material. To critique in such a way fails spectacularly to accept that Kieron 'paints what he sees', nothing more and nothing less. My recommendation is not to question, but to cast aside all senses of doubt or reservation and to simply stand before his work. I trust the pages that follow will serve most adequately to illustrate my somewhat simplistic approach and enable a total appreciation of Kieron's unquestionable skills.

It is the trust and friendship that remains so treasured between our families that lies at the very foundations of Kieron's accomplishments. Where many have supported Kieron on the ladder of success, my son has played a significant role in arranging exhibitions so successfully for Kieron. Adrian was to find himself overseeing the unprecedented interest in Kieron's paintings and at the forefront of monitoring and addressing enquiries from all over the world. He has remained calm and professional throughout and his efficiency has ensured Kieron's best interests continue to be served at every available opportunity.

May you be enchanted by this wonderful account of Kieron's life and his achievements. Find inspiration from the paintings that have been published therein. Above all, may you be continually reminded that you are viewing the work of a remarkable young man on the brink of his 10th birthday.

Michael Hill
PICTURECRAFT of HOLT

'Just Around the Bend' a watercolour of Holt in Norfolk. Kieron's gift to Michael and Teresa Hill with thanks for their support.

ACKNOWLEDGEMENTS

Sincere thanks must go to every member of our family who offered Kieron and Billie-Jo their praise and encouragement and us, their emotional support and unconditional acceptance as events have unfolded over the last few years. Special thanks go to Grandma Gill for her financial help in providing Kieron with the art materials he needed, and for being there for us all. To Mum and Dad, for accompanying us on our first family holiday to Cornwall, where it all started. To uncle Timmy for loaning Kieron his table, which is much loved and used and for Timmy's workmanship on Kieron's house.

To Carol Ann Pennington, artist and gallery owner from The Last Picture Show in Town, who witnessed the ignition of Kieron's interest in art and offered Kieron the first opportunity to explore and display his artwork and for coping with the initial global onslaught. To Michael Hill for sharing with Kieron his passion for the arts, also to Teresa and Clare Hill and especially to Adrian Hill, for his unquestionable patience and sensitive handling of all the enquiries and Kieron's outstanding exhibitions. To young Matt, Val, Bradley, Pete, Graham, Kim, Katie and Charlotte for taking care of us, especially young Billie-Jo during the media events at the Picturecraft Gallery and to Sue, Polly and Helen for their time and patience in Picturecraft's art supplies shop. To Lucy, Mark, Francis and Robert in framing.

To Brian Ryder for inviting Kieron to attend art classes and offering his time and encouragement. To Tony Garner for inviting Kieron to attend art classes and for continuing to offer his time, support and friendship. To Steve Hall for the DVD's. To Rolf Harris for his time and enthusiasm, and continued words of wisdom.

Thanks must also go to Patrick Barkham, from the Guardian for his beautiful articles, his time and shared enthusiasm for nature. To Matt Doughty and team at Boudicca Marketing, for the development of Kieron's website. To Andrew Dibben, for his photographic skills in recording Kieron's artwork and producing the initial prints and images for the book.

To Karen Shoesmith and Jan Sorrell for their invaluable financial advice, patience and encouragement through our darker days. To the team at Hayes & Storr Solicitors for their invaluable legal and ethical advice.

To Beryl Knowles, Simon Walters and the teachers at Holt Primary School for their consistency, encouragement, positivity and for their emotional support.

To Taffy, Kipper, Jess, Honey, and Abby, the dogs who's portrait sales assisted Kieron to pay for his art materials.

To Natalie Gray and Tony the cameraman from Anglia news, for their continued warmth and support. To Caroline and Ray at the Holt Chronicle for celebrating Kieron's work on the front cover. To Karen Bethel for the very first article, and to Alban Donohue for the first iconic photo's. To Tom and Paula, producers at Wall-to-Wall for their patience and humour throughout filming for the Child Genius documentary, Channel 4.

To Mr & Mrs Van-Zeller for taking Kieron to Seago's Dutch House and to meet Jane Seymour. Sincere thanks go to Heather Delf, head teacher for taking us on and to Claire Huke, for bringing the best out of Kieron, working out what makes him tick and helping him to excel, thanks go to everyone at Ludham Primary School and our new neighbours and friends who have made us feel so welcome in the village. To Eric Edwards and the How Hill Trust for welcoming Kieron on site to observe reed cutting first hand.

Thanks must also go to those across the globe, particularly the campers - Adam, Stella, Mark, Liz & Lisa & Rory, who still keep in touch. To the thousands of amazing strangers who email us their own stories and photos, offer us invitations to visit and travel, and who have given us their thanks for sharing Kieron's gift and offer us such heart felt encouragement.

To everyone who has taken the time to visit the Gallery and those who have purchased Kieron's work simply because they love it. Special thanks go to Neil and Jane for their friendship and support.

CONTENTS

Foreword	5
Acknowledgements	6
Introduction	9
Early Light	11
Cornwall 2008	17
The Young Entrepreneur	19
The First Exhibition	31
Sealed Bids	45
Charitable Contributions	51
The Second Exhibition	53
All His Own Work	65
The Third Exhibition	67
What Makes a Child Gifted?	89
Dilemmas	91
The Great Kieron Phenomenon	93
Running Away	95
The Fourth Exhibition	99
Investing for the Future	103
Painting Progress	105
Why Landscapes and Nature?	113
The Fifth Exhibition	115
The Secret to Kieron's Success	121
The Sixth Exhibition: Delamore	123
The Seventh Exhibition	125

'Salthouse', an early oil painting

INTRODUCTION

A happy, energetic boy

Kieron Williamson is a happy, energetic boy, who shares a passion for Leeds United with his father, Keith. He shares with his sister Billie-Jo a fascination for swimming, a love for the trampoline, and the enjoyment of watching *The Simpson's* on television. A culinary delight is roast potatoes, a particular success afforded by his mother, Michelle.

Like most boys of his age Kieron is multi-faceted, giving 200 per cent to everything he undertakes. Evidence of his various activities can usually be found on his clothing. Kieron loves all outdoor pursuits, especially in connection with mud, snow and sand, and he delights in adventures containing all elements of danger. However at the age of five, during the family's first holiday to Cornwall, Kieron had a shift in consciousness. His desire was to 'draw what he saw'. Previously, artistic awareness was simply confined to instructing others to draw dinosaurs for him. Kieron had always been either apprehensive or totally disinterested in drawing anything for himself.

This behavioural change was to lead Kieron and his family on a completely mind-blowing journey. What was expected to be just a 'one-minute-wonder', when a few of his paintings were placed in a window display when he was six years old, laid the foundations for him to develop a successful, globally-recognised career. Kieron's obsession and absolute determination was to continue probing into this newly discovered interest, despite his family's reservations.

Kieron's talent remains a mystery to his parents and to a much wider audience. Some try to attribute an understanding by applying theories such as reincarnation; autism; parental pressure; astrological influences or other articulated misconceptions. Observers fail to appreciate just how much Kieron is in the driving seat. He is acutely aware of the impact that his chosen early career has placed on the shoulders of his parents. Kieron's response is to 'carry on regardless', merely requesting support of his family to assist him in his achievements. Inevitably, this poses many questions and ethical debates by others.

Naturally, it is a very fine balance for the parents of a gifted child to ensure that all the family's needs are met, that a degree of normality is maintained, and that education remains a priority; more importantly, that the child retains their innocence and a strong sense of security. In this instance, the power and determination of a five year old boy, articulate, driven and inspired by the landscapes that surrounded him, set precedence. Such a gift could not be ignored, diverted, suppressed or destroyed.

This enlightening book serves as a true celebration of Kieron Williamson's unquestionable talent, and provides an insight into the awakening and appreciation of his techniques in the three differing media of oil, watercolour and pastel. Albeit at such a young age, the pages that follow offer a chronological account of the action-packed career of East Anglia's youngest artist at this present time. It also provides an honest appreciation of the family's experiences and all the blessings and curses that result from working within such unfamiliar territories.

Children don't arrive with instruction manuals, least of all, immensely talented children.

'Boating', early pastel. "I started off using quite vivid colours but I like the sunset in this picture." KRW

EARLY LIGHT

Michelle Williamson

Kieron was born 4 August 2002 in Norwich, Norfolk. A seventeen hour labour resulted in a touch-and-go emergency caesarean as Kieron was discovered to be a brow presentation. Despite nearly losing him and having two holes in his heart, Kieron went on to show his parents (and the world) exactly what he was made of! He was nicknamed 'King Kieron' at just a few weeks old, somehow able to capture the attention of friends and family. His early years saw him achieve his milestones with ease, and many memories hinge on Kieron's complete determination to succeed. With energy levels that exhausted all those around him, Kieron would prove to be hard work both physically and mentally; his questions were also endless and well illustrated his busy mind.

It is so difficult to know whether you could possibly love a second child as much as you do your first, but the arrival of Billie-Jo on 11 January 2004 proved that it was possible. A completely different character, with different intentions and expectations, Billie has been playmate and chief entertainment's officer for us all. Billie's sunny disposition and carefree pace of life, is not only alien to the rest of us, but is tonic enough, as we have no choice but to join her in her simplistic and totally joyous environment. A lover of sticky tape and scissors, Billie is content and self-assured and thankfully has not a jealous bone in her body, or any desires to achieve the same accolade as Kieron. Billie has been such great support, in fact none of this could happen if it wasn't for her unconditional acceptance and tolerance. She is so proud of Kieron and his artwork; she duly recognises why people are interested in it. Billie is thrilled at being beside Kieron during the various media events and has thoroughly enjoyed the trips to London that Kieron's fame has offered. There were never any fights or issues between the children as a result of Kieron's artwork, even Kieron's dominance over the kitchen table was accepted and Billie improvised; she completely filled the bedroom that they shared, with toys, tables, dolls and paper.

Between 2002–2011 home was in Holt, Norfolk; a two- bedroomed first-floor flat that overlooked a garage forecourt. The lack of garden space saw the bath as being one of the main attractions. If water play was not organised for Kieron, he would simply do it himself and play in the bath fully clothed. Pre-school offered Kieron the delights of a sandpit, but encouraging Kieron to do anything other than play in the sand was a challenge. Table top and group activities were not appealing to him unless dinosaur-related, so painting became relevant as he mixed jungle and desert sand colours together. Kieron would participate in art and craft activities at home, but only for short spans of time; there was always something more pressing to do. Before starting school, Kieron had learned the names of numerous dinosaurs and would group them into families and herds in amongst his train set. A passion for tractors and emergency vehicles also offered sufficient entertainment. As a toddler Kieron's favourite colour was black and he would paint whole sheets of paper in thick black paint. A momentary cause for concern, but there was nothing in Kieron's development that suggested he was different in any way.

The arrival of the house cats in 2006, Burmese brother and sister Shooi and Evie, was to release a gutsy laugh from Kieron, who had previously been rather conservative with his expressions. Kieron relished in watching the cats' playful abandonment and risk taking. Other activities much loved by Kieron were sliding down the stairs on large sheets of cardboard, riding his tractor around

Kieron aged 4

'Barn and Poppies', an early oil

'Light and Shade Over Barns', an early oil

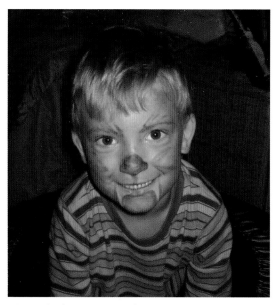

Kieron in face paint aged 5

A fondness for animals

Kieron and Billie-Jo with Keith

in the snow, and pond dipping at the local stream. It was essential to get the children out for air and exercise, and Kieron perhaps saw the big outdoors more often than his peers. Keen on wildfowl, wildlife and mud, the opportunities to see these things were frequent. Bedtimes would provide a rough and tumble on the lounge floor, followed by a race to the bedroom, Kieron on dad's shoulders, and Billie in mum's arms, to see who could get into bed first.

Kieron attended the local nurseries and Primary school in Holt and, despite not wanting to go, he managed to get a great deal out of it. Kieron was never difficult to get through the doors, but given the choice of going to school, or staying at home, to be king of his own castle, he would have chosen home. Holt Primary school was to offer Kieron a level of encouragement and enthusiasm for learning that appealed to his desire to achieve. A few local colouring competitions and sports day achievements were huge successes that added to Kieron's sense of pride and fuelled his search for other avenues to achieve results, and the school's football team saw Kieron enrolled early at age seven.

Weekends were spent riding bikes alongside dad, playing football at the park or walking to Letheringsett ford. But 2007 was to see Kieron's dad sustain a nasty achilles rupture, making all outdoor activities a thing of the past. There were other obvious and painful losses; rough and tumbles stopped, the race to bed stopped. These were replaced with reading and times tables' practice, a new partnership that would allow the boys their time together but in a different, learning-centred fashion. Keith's recovery was long and difficult, as well as problematic; DVT and Complex Regional Pain Syndrome were diagnosed and brought with them their own challenges. I was busy studying, trying to return to work, and suffering with agoraphobia and fatigue meant that indoor pursuits were the only option outside the normal routine of school.

'Towards the Sea', early pastel. "I love painting muddy estuaries. I don't think this will ever change." KRW

'Factory' - an early crayon and charcoal drawing

To mention here the affliction of having two depressed parents, each with health issues is important, because we have been criticised for engineering our son's early career in art. It is true to say that we were too self-absorbed with our own issues to be even remotely interested in the children's careers, after all, they were only five and six years old. Living with depression forces you to look for the source of light in each day, whether it is a child's laugh, a job well done, or simply a day with fewer complaints, it was easy for us to encourage the children to seek activities that inspired them and engaged their creativity. These things were free, achievable and necessary. It was also important for us to find an avenue where we were more comfortable, for Keith it was the exploration of developing his hobby of buying artwork at auction into a possible viable business having been told that he couldn't return to the building trade. For me it was the challenge of justifying my time at home raising a family, with coursework and efforts to return to work to shake off the post natal depression. I am amazed we survived those times, and out of that, grew a talent so wonderful; why didn't Kieron have behaviour issues instead?

Painting on the marshes

'Low Tide', early pastel. "I was taught basic principles on how to create depth in a picture. I like to see creeks disappear into the scene." KRW

CORNWALL 2008

The holiday to Cornwall and Devon in May 2008 was significant for many different reasons; it was the family's first ever holiday, and after eight long months of recovery and rehabilitation, it was long overdue. It allowed the family the time outside again, enjoying the picture-perfect views of fishing villages and harbour towns. With Grandparents in tow, it was easy to soak up the atmosphere. A small bay near to Gillan provided the boys with evening walks, offering Kieron the chance to smell the sea and breathe in the Cornish spirit. Kieron asked us to buy him a drawing pad, he wanted to 'draw what he saw' and despite this being so very out of character, we duly obliged. And so equipped with his pad and Billie's colouring pencils, Kieron routinely visited the bay. The following morning we assumed Kieron had gone to watch TV, but an hour or two later, he returned to the kitchen to show us his picture page filled with sky, sea, boats. We were amazed and offered the much deserved praise and recognition.

Kieron and Billie-Jo in Cornwall

One of Kieron's drawings made during the holiday in Cornwall in May 2008.

Kieron had changed, but it is only now looking back to that time, that we see more clearly just how much he had changed. Back then, we assumed, he was missing his toys and was trying to fill his time with activity, now we see the conscious decision he made at that time to employ drawing as his primary pastime, and just how determined he was to be a landscape painter. Each day that followed provided him with opportunities to survey the landscape around him and the small steps towards Kieron forming his own boats and harbours. We naturally assumed that when Kieron returned home to a normal routine, that he would forget the drawing, but he proved us wrong, and has continued to prove us wrong every day since.

'Would you like to see the pictures I did on holiday?' Kieron asked as he shyly stood by the door of my office – not an unusual request as many of my pupils liked to show me things they had done during the holidays. The pictures (a result of the Williamson family's first trip to Cornwall) were lovely – light, impressionistic and surprisingly good for a five year old. In response to this interest, I pulled a couple of books off my shelf – I think they were called 'How to Draw' and 'A Guide to Painting'. Subsequent events have made me blush at this attempt to teach Kieron how to do what he clearly does so well! **Beryl Knowles, teacher**

Kieron at Gillan, Cornwall 2008

Kieron, Billie-Jo and Keith, Cornwall 2008

Kieron's drawing made at Gillan in Cornwall in May 2008. 'I loved the small bay in Cornwall, and I wanted to capture the boats and the sky." KRW

THE YOUNG ENTREPRENEUR

Keith and I began to collect original paintings in 2002, we loved the honesty in the works of Jack Cox and the freedom seen in the work of Hugh Brandon-Cox, and our walls were peppered with paintings. Kieron's baby record acknowledges that at 12 months, he would look at the paintings along the landing and gesture towards them. He would know instantly if paintings had been moved or swapped about. Kieron loved the idea of seeing scenes of Wells and Blakeney on our walls and then being able to go to these places and experience them in the flesh, and throughout the different seasons. Kieron used to accompany us to local the galleries at times when we had popped in for a chat, or to look at the recent change in works. But Kieron's time in the gallery was brief, interrupted by the urge to do a few circuits in the car park outside; a flash of blue would skip past the doorway letting you know he was still in the area. The attention he paid to the artwork was however to expand over time, gradually and unconsciously, progressing from making animal noises and uttering 'boat' or 'horse' at the appropriate subject, to comments on the colours, composition, subject matter and other people's contributions on the same.

'Kipper', Kieron's first formal pet portrait

An early acrylic. "I love autumn shades and muddy lanes, inspired by the artist Kevin Curtis who painted real mud." KRW

Pet portraits, left to right: 'Jess' (acrylic), 'Taffy' (acrylic), and 'Abby' (oil)

Happy-go-lucky, Kieron with his sister Billie-Jo

To say that Kieron hit the accelerator pedal in his learning about art is an understatement. I cannot sufficiently describe in words how Kieron filled each minute of the day from the age of five, learning, practicing, drawing and discovering. He insisted on using artist-quality materials, which we discovered were not cheap given how prolific 2008 and 2009 proved to be. Kieron's thirst for knowledge soon out-ran us, and we began to rely upon the help and support of local gallery owners and artists to provide the technical answers that Kieron sought. The galleries were welcoming, friendly and enthusiastic, and the time that they offered Kieron was astonishing, and truly appreciated, although at times we did wonder whether Kieron was actually listening or not, his trade mark 'uh ums' offered no guarantee that he was paying attention, but his actions and progress did. Kieron was a sponge for information, insight and understanding, and this was rewarded. An invitation to join a local adult watercolour class held by Brian Ryder ROI for nine weeks, and an introduction to oil painting for three weeks, kindly sponsored by the Picturecraft Gallery, witnessed Kieron holding his own alongside his adult peers.

Light-hearted moments and young children in art galleries are not necessarily associated. As Kieron became older, and much more vocal, he would often come and advise me that he had identified his favourite painting in the gallery. We would then find ways to establish the reasoning of his choice and then take time to make comparisons and to study carefully other works on display. He would make surprisingly mature choices and enjoyed justifying his selected picture with solid reasoning, sometimes indicating that the texture of the painting had influenced his opinion. Once fully satisfied that he had offered a reasonable explanation of his critique, he would seek approval to go and have a run around. Just as any normal, happy-go-lucky child of his years would do, he would race around outside on the large shingle area in front of the gallery, confident in convincing us all that he was getting faster and faster every time he visited the gallery. **Adrian Hill, Picturecraft Gallery**

An early pastel. "I like adding distant figures and dogs to my work." KRW

An early pastel. "I completed this pastel while I was in the Picturecraft Gallery one day with Tony Garner."
KRW

An early oil. "Big Norfolk Skies are important I think. I like this lane disappearing." KRW

Kieron's portrait of his sister, Billie-Jo

I was rather concerned that a 10-week art course for adults would prove far too advanced and especially tiring for six-year old Kieron at the end of a busy school week. How wrong could I have been! Always the first to arrive and the last to leave each week, Kieron had the entire class totally captivated by his ability to grasp this tuition. Accompanied by his mother every week, Michelle would take notes on Kieron's behalf. Notes however proved incidental in his wonderful ability to watch, listen and learn, and to put this valuable instruction immediately into use in order to produce beautiful paintings in watercolour and ink and wash. Never phased or hampered by constraint, Kieron revealed an expressive painting technique at a level of energy and speed beyond comprehension. The guidance from Brian Ryder was appreciated above measure and enabled Kieron to approach and concentrate on techniques in watercolour painting with confidence and new levels of ability.

Perhaps what always amazed me was what happened after the art class. Kieron would walk home with his mother, enthusing all the way about the knowledge he had gained from the class. Without exception, before anyone else had risen in his household the following morning, Kieron would undertake another version of the painting from the art class and this would be ready for the rest of the family to see at breakfast. This painting not only demonstrated a total understanding of the techniques absorbed from the night before but allowed him to develop his own personal style. Kieron's second attempt would show accomplished and quite distinct levels of impressionism, but always with a solid underpinning of realism. He was already starting to overcome, 'beginner's problems' with watercolour painting, something that can take considerable time to achieve and fondly referred to in painting terms as, 'freeing up'.

Each Saturday, Kieron would proudly bring this newly completed painting into the gallery for me to see. Having experienced the struggle of painting this picture for myself in the art class, I was always eager to see Kieron's own personal interpretation. We often referred to this as a painting being, 'Kieronised'. I can recall one particular evening at the art class sitting at the back of the room sharing a table with my father. We were both struggling to come to terms with the challenge of drawing a boat. We were suddenly aware of a little head appearing in between us and Kieron's grin as he studied our two paintings. Turning his attention to me he politely enquired, "Have you ever done a good painting Mr Hill?" To which I responded, "Have you come to show me how to do it then?" The immediacy of the challenge was far too great for Kieron. Seizing my pencil he presented me with two perfect little boats drawn to scale at the bottom of my painting, and in seconds was back at the front of the class eagerly awaiting further instruction from the tutor.

My father was to also come across the 'helping hand of Kieron' during one of our art classes. The concept of mixing the correct tone in watercolour for shadows had been thoroughly explained. We had all been told that mixing too much red would prove too hot, and too much blue would result in the shadow being too cool. It was essential that exactly the correct amount of watercolour was used. Our task was to complete our landscape painting by applying a watercolour wash which would give the impression of a deep shadow cast across the foreground. Nervously, we all commenced mixing our shadow colour, but Kieron had already successfully accomplished his mixing and finished his painting to great effect. My father was busy mixing his paints, appearing to be in great difficulty in achieving the correct tone. Occasionally he found it necessary to test his colour on a spare piece of watercolour paper. Suddenly a voice came from behind my father, "Too hot Mr Hill, far too much red!" **Adrian Hill**

Inset: Kieron with Brian Ryder ROI

Holt in Norfolk figured in many of Kieron's earliest works

Another invitation to attend pastel classes with pastel artist Tony Garner continued Kieron's opportunities to learn alongside other adults until he realised that he wanted to work at a faster pace to the rest of the class. The last class was to witness Kieron work on two pictures within the same time frame.

Time with Tony was to continue, and it spilled into fishing, painting oils on location, and talking about football. Tony remains on hand for the swapping of photos, the odd email, text and question from Kieron, to which Tony willingly responds with all the love, affection and mutual respect you'd expect between any close friends.

An early acrylic. "I painted this on unstretched canvas, using quite a dilute acrylic paint." KRW

An early acrylic. "Acrylics are not so easy to blend, and trying to achieve natural shades is sometimes difficult." KRW

An early acrylic. "I love the snow and crisp blue colours in this picture." KRW

An early acrylic. "Most of my early work had an horizon." KRW

Kieron working with Tony Garner in the gallery

Kieron working alongside Tony Garner at Kelling, Norfolk

Teaching the Aspiring Artist

In 2009 I was due to do a pastel demonstration at the Picturecraft Gallery in Holt, North Norfolk. I was asked by the proprietor if a very young artist could come and watch me work. I agreed and on the day of the demonstration I was setting up my easel when a man, whom I recognised as a regular visitor to the gallery, entered with a very small boy.

After a quick introduction I started to work. The young man drew a little, rummaged around in my pastel tray, went into the corner of the gallery where he announced that he was going to copy a picture that was being exhibited at that time. He sat with legs crossed and proceeded to work. Within no time at all he had put down his pencil and disappeared into the car park. After a few circuits of the park he returned, looking like any self-respecting boy should look; dirty and muddy! He continued to work and watch with silent yet great enthusiasm until his father decided it was time to leave. Suddenly the whirlwind had gone and feeling slightly shell shocked I sat and tried to compose myself. Little did I know that I was lucky enough to be present at the start of a remarkable journey.

I offered to help, however I could, as my way of 'putting something back' in helping develop the skills required in this fledgling career. Kieron started attending my workshops and quickly proved that he had something very special.

I have taught many aspiring artists, who have usually seemed to want to exactly replicate my techniques and in so doing have produced work which has been similar to my own. Not so Kieron. He has watched, copied and then 'Kieronised' the work. He has always had a clear understanding way beyond his years and has his own way of expressing himself. We do not talk much about perspective, or tone or indeed composition, and I am always mindful of the fact that he should not be pushed in any particular direction. My role is merely to help, if asked. More often than not it is with matters of a practical nature such as what materials to use, how to prepare them for the best results and perhaps the odd critique.

Once, when I first started to paint, I was on the wrong end of a very bad critique and as such I went home, put away my brushes and felt quite worthless. Suffice it to say that I have always been very careful to find the good in someone's work, if asked. None of us get it right all the time and so my way is to encourage Kieron and pick out the pieces that have worked particularly well.

It is not all work however. I remember we were out painting one day and had a couple of rather nice pieces of chocolate cherry cake. The importance of the attributes of the landscape before us, paled into insignificance when compared to the argument that raged between us as to who had the most cherries in their slice.

In short, my relationship with Kieron is more of a friendship which extends to all of his family, particularly his ever-smiling sister Billie-Jo who, incidentally, is a better fisherman than her brother.

Kieron is quite simply quiet, shy yet self-assured and unbelievably enthusiastic about committing to canvas all of the things that surround him. His work is fresh, vigorous, and spontaneous and displays a vibrancy and quality that is commendable in someone of such a tender age. I look upon him as the grandson I never had and hope that he continues to be successful for as long as he wishes to paint. There is much more to come. **Tony Garner**

Somehow when family members willingly handed over £5 for one of Kieron's pictures, Kieron knew he was on to a good thing! Kieron's advert in the *Holt Chronicle* to sell pet portraits for pocket money to help buy his art materials led to a phenomenal local response, too big for the six year old to commit to. Kieron also compiled a list of top ten tips on being 'young at art'! Just as other artists had been happy to share their techniques, Kieron showed the same willingness to share. Kieron was in the zone, painting, creating, practicing, experimenting, and loving every minute.

An early pastel. "This pastel shows a lot of painting principles: light, shade, movement in the water, creating depth and distance, clouds being darker at the base." KRW

An early pastel. "2009 was quite a busy year and saw the use of oils, watercolours and pastels." KRW

An early pastel. "Trying to create movement and a 3D effect in the sails was quite tricky." KRW

THE FIRST EXHIBITION

Holt was to hold its first festival in 2009. But for the local population, few of the activities were 'home-grown'. A polar bear was to visit the streets along with several other imported acts. Although the event was to do well for the town and prove to be very popular, we didn't feel that it reflected the true spirit of the residents of Holt. As proud parents, too afraid to approach the festival organisers for an opportunity to show Kieron's work through fear of being laughed at, we spoke with Carol Ann Pennington, artist and gallery owner. Carol was surprised at the lack of child-centred activities, and warmly welcomed the opportunity to show Kieron's paintings in her side window during festival week. Carol had been kind enough to offer Kieron weekly art sessions before she opened her gallery during the summer holidays of 2008. Carol had also been surprised by Kieron's new-found hobby and could see that Kieron was developing quite a 'tight' style to his artwork, by that I mean, very detailed and precise, even at that young age.

'Marshland Cattle' - an oil exhibited at Kieron's first exhibition. 'I like this painting because it has a nice atmosphere.' KRW

First exhibition: 'Norfolk Barn and Cattle'. "The mud and the barn are the most important pieces in this picture, but I also like the misty sky." KRW

'Cattle on the Marsh' - oil on canvas shown at Kieron's first exhibition

Carol's work is beautiful, bright and contemporary, and I think she wanted to show Kieron that art could be fun, colourful, and abstract at times. Kieron enjoyed his hour-long sessions and the subsequent homework. Kieron was set the task of mixing different shades of grey. When he returned to Carol's studio the following week, he humbly produced a sheet of over 30 shades of grey, and further discussions with Kieron identified the uses that each shade would offer in particular paintings. Colour mixing for Kieron was an innate ability, at times he doesn't even look at the palette when he's painting. The Festival Week of 2009 did not permit Carol to offer the same tutoring commitment, so we happily accepted the window space to show Kieron's progress that he'd achieved throughout the year.

We were delighted and overwhelmed at the chance to celebrate Kieron's work with a small window display. We had arranged for Grandma and a family friend to go to the gallery and purchase their pet portraits, to allow Kieron to experience the 'sale' of his work. We never imagined for a second that people would want to buy it. The 19 paintings were a mix of watercolours, acrylics, and early oil paintings. We soon learned that the watercolours were to be framed for Kieron, again free of charge by Michael and Teresa Hill at the Picturecraft Gallery. We were so humbled, and embarrassed I think, at the time and effort that other people were putting into Kieron's work. I don't think even then, that we realised what talent Kieron had. We didn't see him as being any different, just very fortunate to have had the support offered to him by the galleries. We certainly didn't see Kieron as being prodigious, or above his peers in his artwork; we never thought either that he would carry on with it, so the thought of him becoming an established artist when he was older just didn't enter our heads.

First exhibition: 'Morston Creek, towards Blakeney'. watercolour

Recollections of Kieron's First Exhibition

I had met Keith and Michelle in early 2002 and witnessed the arrival and early development of both Kieron and his sister Billie-Jo. Kieron was usually 50 yards in front either on his way to nursery or to the park. Who could have guessed then that the lives of their young family could change overnight into a helterskelter of events which most of us would have found impossible to control and manage.

It was Kieron who at five years of age came to our Studio/Gallery throughout the summer holidays of 2008, very early in the morning before I opened to the public. Kieron's desire to 'learn about using colour' and putting paint on canvas had coincided with his father's ruptured achilles tendon. (It is worth remarking upon the limitations of the family home which had no garden and two very active children under the age of six.) For Kieron to have one-to-one attention and teaching for an hour at the Last Picture Show did much to alleviate the situation. No one at this stage was prepared for what was to develop from these sessions.

For the first 45 minutes Kieron would absorb and retain all I could teach him about colour mixing, perspective and shape. The final 15 minutes were left for him to use in any way he wished. I remember being 'disappointed' when he chose constantly to produce the traditional landscapes familiar to him, rather than embarking with a bright palette on new experimental abstracts. How wrong can one be.? What he chose to paint is now coveted by collectors the world over. I also remember being amazed that when this earnest young child experimented with the greys, blues and greens of his palette in the colour mixing exercises, he mixed an incredibly wide range of shades, all minimally different, then more amazingly knew exactly which hue he would select and mix for works produced in subsequent weeks clearly remembering how he had created them. I took these early studies home and only the fact that I had witnessed the creation of them from start to finish convinced Tony, my husband (a Child Psychologist), that they had in fact come directly from the eye, hand and heart of this young artist.

Later when the National Press first became involved in 'Kieron's Story' many more people were to doubt and question the authenticity of this early work.

Kieron's first exhibition, which we held here at the Last Picture Show to coincide with The Holt Festival 2009 consisted of a variety of landscapes painted during that period, both in our gallery and at home. Many were unframed canvases, while others, on watercolour paper were framed by Picturecraft, another local gallery who on seeing the works thought our local press might be interested

'Honey' an acrylic for the first exhibition

Kieron with Carol Pennington

enough to include copies in their Festival Issue. What happened next was phenomenal. People came from far and wide, some were sceptical, others openly envious; the majority rejoicing with sincere appreciation of what they saw.

The National Press and Television descended upon us requiring proof that this was a real story, and throughout that first heady week Michelle and I spent hours fielding questions from the press on 'the three A's' at the heart of this global debate – Authenticity, Autism, Art. Kieron himself, in his totally unselfconscious way was to defend the integrity of all who were initially involved Totally unfazed by demands for him to 'perform' and produce a piece of art in front of camera and live audiences he embarked upon a succession of interviews, which clearly showed then, and have continued to the present time to show, that he loves what he does and that he can do it whatever his surroundings. What he sees he puts down on paper or canvas.

Kieron is not *autistic* but *artistic* in all that he seeks to create. He, now at 9 years old, has an impressive range of skills that were guided by a handful of local artists who since that first exhibition have offered their various specialisms in furthering his career. Now self-assured, quietly confident and deeply determined to rise above the frustrations that continue to surround his space, Kieron continues to do what he loves, and is supported wholeheartedly by his family.

Kieron Williamson, when his brushes are cleaned ready for the morrow will rush off to the football pitch (where again he excels), throw himself wholeheartedly into the physical hurly-burly with joyful abandon. He will return dirty, hot and hungry for his tea, just like any other 9 year old.

His family life is no longer simple, but their resolve to protect themselves and both children from the exploitation and greed which come as bedfellow to the glory, has often pushed them to the limits of patience. Time spent with Michelle and the children has seen them agonise at times over the commercial issues that accompany this story. There is no going back to how things were before. What lies ahead is unfathomable. Somewhere in between must be a balance.

At home I have a Christmas card from Kieron made when he was five It has a bright red robin perched on a twig and, yes, in the mature draftsmanship there are signs of what was come. Alongside this is a card from Billie-Jo his younger sister, again of a robin on a twig. The very typical work of a three and a half year old. Tony and I treasure them both equally. They were executed with both enthusiasm and care, then sent with love. At the end of the day that is all that matters. **Carol Pennington**

First exhibition: 'Sailing Wherry at Sunset', acrylic

First exhibition: 'Figures on a Bridge'. watercolour.
"I love the wet into wet effect in the trees." KRW

'Barn Owl' painted by Kieron as a gift
for his teacher, Beryl Knowles.

Kieron at School

When the interest began to grow in Kieron's work and family life, we made a conscious decision at school – our job was not about his talent for art – our job was to keep him 'rounded and grounded'. We were worried that Kieron might get bullied because of his talent but his personal integrity, unusual in one so young, made our fears groundless. Kieron's passion for football is well known – as soon as he was in Y3 (and out on the 'big playground') break and lunchtimes became opportunities for football. The children played together, irrespective of age and size but few children as young as Kieron were wholeheartedly accepted and encouraged by the older pupils – Kieron was in demand by both teams and I don't think it was anything to do with how well he could paint. **Beryl Knowles**

An article featured in the *North Norfolk News* and the *EDP*, July 2009, describing Kieron's appreciation for art, and it changed our lives. Upon leaving the house, Keith laughed to himself and imagined the film crews arriving, but at that exact moment we opened our front door to Natalie Gray from Anglia News!

This interview was followed by photographers, newspapers and news channels, trips to the Forum in Norwich and to London, it suddenly dawned on us what Kieron had achieved at the age of 6 and 7, but we never imagined it would happen to us.

Members of the public flocked to Holt to see the display, and to enjoy the festival activities. We skulked among the evening shadows of town in hats to get fresh air and exercise. Poor Carol was inundated, 30-40 enquiries a day, plus visitors. We were overwhelmed with the support shown to us on a local level, let alone support from all over the world. It's still a treat to read emails from around the globe, children choosing Kieron as their school project, and school magazines wanting to use Kieron to promote artwork in the classroom.

First exhibition: 'Snow Scene'. watercolour 'I love the shadows increasing the chill factor of the snow.' KRW

Media Attention Grows

I was most surprised to discover the six-year-old boy from the small town of Holt then featuring on the BBC National News at 10pm. Within just a few hours this local news story was now reaching into homes throughout the United Kingdom. It was a truly humbling experience to have my relatively small role of encouragement acknowledged, but I was excited for Kieron. So many people had now been made aware of the talents of this remarkable little boy... and I found myself pondering over what tomorrow would bring, for this was the first day that the paintings were going to be placed on show to the public .

Newspapers continued to express interest in the hopes of meeting and featuring this exciting new child prodigy, and pressure was continually mounting trying to establish whether any of the paintings were for sale, inevitably followed by the only remaining unanswered question, "What is the price of a Kieron Williamson painting?" **Adrian Hill**

First exhibition: 'Cornish Beach with Fishermen.' acrylic. "I like the movement in the water in this painting." KRW

First exhibition: 'Cornish Fishing Boat, Lighthouse, and Gulls.' acrylic."The reflection in this painting balances the warm shades with the cool." KRW

First exhibition: 'Church', watercolour. "I like the light and shadows being cast in this painting." KRW

First exhibition: 'Cows at Salthouse', watercolour

First exhibition: 'Holkham Beach', watercolour

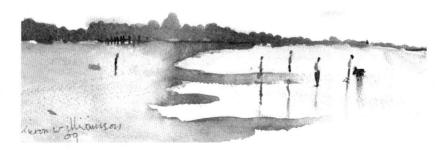

First exhibition: 'Reedcutters at Cley', oil, inspired by Jeremy Barlow ROI. "I love the simplicity of this piece." KRW

First exhibition: 'North Norfolk Landscape', oil

First exhibition: 'Morston Creek, towards Blakeney', oil

SEALED BIDS

How do you place a value on the work of a six year old? We never intended to sell the work, the display contained two pet portraits for family and friends and Keith's father's day present! People were asking how they could buy Kieron's paintings and it was decided that sealed bids from the public was a fair process, so that people could pay what they wanted, and assess the value of the work themselves. Each and every painting in the display had tags placed on them and bids were left. Kieron was happy to sell the work and so we were happy too, surprised, and overwhelmed at the speed at which events were occurring.

Thankfully friends have since said that, given the same circumstances, they would have made the same decision. Such decisions bring with them the heaviest of ethical debates, this is my family and my little boy in the middle of all this, and I felt completely overwhelmed, scared, excited, happy, exposed, and fearful. I don't know how else to describe the state Keith and I were in. It was like slipping into a parallel life. Kieron, however, enjoyed the fact that people were coming to Holt to look at his work and wanted to buy it; his perception of events was so different from ours. It was important to us that people saw without doubt that it was Kieron's own work. It was easy for Kieron to offer people that assurance, and the scepticism was incredibly short lived. We were so proud of

'Winter', a favourite pastel, sold at the first Picture-craft Gallery exhibition

'Blakeney', art class piece with Brian Ryder ROI, sold at the first exhibition . "I love the clouds and colours in this piece, I enjoyed painting it." KRW.

A Son First, Artist Second

At school, Kieron was 'into everything' – an enthusiastic learner who was able to balance a serious attitude with a definite fun side. This contrast between a rather reserved boy and the bold, confident artist is fascinating. Kieron rose to every challenge; building his stamina by running through the churchyard on his way to school and improving his maths by learning his times tables. Kieron was well liked by his classmates – I never saw him fall out with anyone, no mean feat in a primary school classroom. He is a natural leader without appearing to lead. Willing to get on with whatever we asked, Kieron sounds like a model pupil – he was, even though for much of the time, he would have preferred to be at home. It would have been easy for Michelle and Keith to put school in second place behind the huge demands that Kieron's talents placed on the family, but they were always keen to see Kieron as a 'whole child' – their son first, an artist second. **Beryl Knowles**

Kieron painting in Norfolk

him, so pleased that he had the strength of character at such a young age to perform live and in front of cameras. Like any other six year old, Kieron offered one syllable answers to questions, but to accept the numerous media projects illustrated how mature and determined he was. He was changing in front of our eyes, coping and in control, enjoying the circus.

Of course we met scepticism, judgement, and criticism, it was an extraordinary story, and looking at the work, we could understand people's doubts. We had seen Kieron's work progress over the year, so it wasn't as surprising to us as it was to those seeing Kieron's work for the first time. I think it's hard for parents with children of a similar age to appreciate how much Kieron is in control, and the extent of his expectations on us to support him. Kieron's willingness to paint in front of people has seen him paint for TV channels all over the world.

* * *

We are often quizzed as to whether Kieron is forced to paint. It's difficult to convince people because most boys are fighting in the dirt, playing console games, football, or riding their bikes around town. Kieron honestly chooses what he paints and when he paints. As a Leo, you couldn't get Kieron to do anything he didn't want to do. He spent two months recently without picking up a brush or a pencil. He is very much in the driving seat of this whole scenario; he knows where he wants to go and expects us to support him. It's quite a challenge to put our responsibilities on hold to prioritise Kieron's hobby, and we tell ourselves that the global interest won't continue, the novelty will wear off, we can return to normal, but as yet that hasn't happened. Kieron has achieved this status within three years. We have cancelled so many other media events, trips, interviews and London exhibitions, so it is mind numbing to wonder where we could be. If we were doing this for the money, we would have taken up those invitations to exhibit in London, Hong Kong, New York, Australia and Germany. Kieron doesn't endure a daily painting regime, or weekly timetable, he is free as a bird to dip into it as often as the inspiration calls.

'A Cold Snap', oil, a painting auctioned online

'Blickling Lake, Norfolk', pastel, a
painting auctioned online

'Incoming Light', oil, a painting auctioned online

Kieron's painting for the 'Art for Starlight' charity auction in 2009

Below: Kieron's contribution to the Postcard charity auction at The Little Theatre, Sheringham, Norfolk

Above: Kieron and Carrie Grant painting on location. Their paintings were auctioned for Children in Need in 2010.

Below: Kieron and Billie-Jo at the Starlight Foundation event in the Saatchi Gallery, 2009

CHARITABLE CONTRIBUTIONS

You cannot read about your son in the papers without being affected by the parallel stories that feature at that same moment in time, and as a result of Kieron's early success, we were invited to attend Holt Rotary Club to offer a painting demonstration, and then to a celebrity art auction at the Saatchi Gallery, London in Sept 2009. It was an immense occasion, attended by Kate Middleton and Prince William. Kieron's star shaped canvas was to raise £6000 for charity.

Each year Kieron has chosen a worthy cause to support, and has offered either paintings for auction or a percentage of his raised funds to help others less fortunate. 2010 saw Kieron offer a painting demonstration for the Swaffham Rotary Club and contributions to DebRA and Children in Need. 2011 supported St Luke's Hospice, Plymouth. In 2012 Kieron supported the RNLI at the Delamore Arts exhibition in Devon and the Norfolk Wildlife Trust. Help for Heroes was supported at the Kieron's seventh exhibition in July 2012. Along with offering charitable contributions, Kieron pays tax ten years before his peers will be expected to.

'Cattle on the Marshes' oil, sold at Kieron's second exhibition. "This was the inspiration behind the star canvas I completed for charity." KRW

'Delamore House', watercolour. Exhibited at the 2011 Delamore Arts Exhibition raising funds for St Luke's Hospice, Plymouth

THE SECOND EXHIBITION

The Picturecraft Gallery came to the rescue with managing the sealed bids for the first exhibition and enthusiastically offered a bay rental to Kieron for his birthday. This saw the setup of a fast approaching November exhibition. A total of 16 paintings were exhibited.

After dropping the children off to school I went to the gallery; the car park was unexpectedly quiet and I thought that maybe it would take the two months to sell the artwork, given that we had not advertised the event. When I entered the gallery and looked at the display, a sea of red presented itself, all 16 paintings showed sold stickers and had sold within minutes. Wow! It was surreal. We phoned the school to let Kieron know his work had sold, he had been preoccupied with the exhibition and balancing that and school was frustrating for him.

'Lone Boat', oil, sold at Kieron's second exhibition

'Sunset at Cley, Norfolk', oil, sold at Kieron's second exhibition. "I'm so glad that I could achieve a sunset in oil.". KRW

'Opposite: 'Windmill at Sunset', pastel, sold at Kieron's second exhibition

'First Snow', pastel, sold at Kieron's second exhibition. *Adrian Hill recalls* "Once Kieron had been summoned to the telephone he opened the conversation by asking, not if anything had sold, but, 'Did the people like my paintings?'. We all struggled to hold back the tears that morning."

'Holkham Beach', pastel, sold at Kieron's second exhibition

I was kindly invited to the Williamson home to peruse the latest works and was to find myself totally overwhelmed with Kieron's rapid advancement. The paintings revealed an incredible maturity in all three mediums of watercolour, oil and pastel. Not only was Kieron producing his own interpretations from photographs and sketches that had been undertaken when venturing out to places in North Norfolk with his family, but he was showing that he had the ability to handle almost any subject with a great degree of confidence. I recall carefully studying a painting of Pin Mill in Suffolk where Kieron had included a most striking flash of blue against the background. This bold mark led you into the painting and had significantly enhanced the overall construction in becoming an incidental, but highly important, focal point. The unexplained use and random placing of such a vibrant colour featured in no other part of the painting. Kieron didn't know why he had used it, but knew that the painting was deserving of it and was happy in the way it had worked. I was immediately struck by these early signals of professionalism from this extraordinary seven year old.

Kieron's favourite pastel, sold at his second exhibition

*   *   *

The question of pricing Kieron's paintings was raised once again. The sealed bid process worked well for those who were happy to accept the terms of sale for bidding online, but the enormous amount of administration work and the legal issues involved in operating such a system had left an undesirable taste. I was keen to adopt a much more straightforward approach to selling Kieron's paintings, and Keith and Michelle endorsed that they would both feel much more comfortable with an easier arrangement too. I confessed to have given very little thought to the implications of how it felt for them selling their son's work, but my responsibility was to do my very best for Kieron. My suggestion was that the paintings should be offered for sale at a determined amount and sold on a first-come- first-served basis. Where this was overwhelmingly received with united approval I was soon to discover, to everyone's amusement, that the task of pricing the paintings was to be my responsibility!

I was acutely aware that this was going to be an unprecedented opportunity for my gallery, given that interest in Kieron's progression from the media was still at an extraordinarily high level. I made arrangements to add a portfolio on to my website which would reveal the sixteen works that were going to be exhibited in November. I had amassed literally hundreds of email addresses from interested people from all around the world who had indicated that they would love to receive more information in connection with Kieron's paintings. My initial task was to try and enlighten them all that an exhibition was going to take place in November and that details were on my website. I spent considerable time working in the evenings from a very modest computer system to ensure that everyone who had registered their interest was informed. It was immediately apparent that sixteen paintings were certainly not going to satisfy such enormous demand. However, I could not possibly place further demands on Kieron. Of utmost importance, and a situation that has remained in place to this day, was to ensure that this little boy could have the complete freedom to paint only when he wanted to.

Kieron seemed oblivious to what was going on... almost to the point of disinterest. He was racing around the gallery with his sister, Billie-Jo, and had found a large brown piece of wrapping paper which was quickly fashioned in a temporary football. My father helped me with the final hanging of the paintings, but frequently found himself distracted when the 'paper football' lunged his way, much to the great amusement of Kieron and Billie-Jo! Despite the seriousness of the situation, the atmosphere was relaxed for Kieron and he was having great fun, something that I felt was vitally important at that time.

The first exhibition for Kieron Williamson at Picturecraft was finally ready. The paintings were priced and the scene was set for the following morning. As a special treat, Kieron's Great-Grandad and his proud Grandparents were ushered into the gallery for a sneak preview during the evening. It was an emotional time, there were a few tears and a great sense of pride and admiration. **Adrian Hill**

Something very big was happening to us, we didn't understand it the first time and the second time didn't make things any clearer for us. We had only contacted people on Kieron's mailing list, there had not been any media coverage or publicity prior to the exhibition, we certainly didn't expect a repeat performance, and so the sales were just to people on the phone and internet. The media soon woke up to the story and we were again doing interviews back to back.

'Brancaster', pastel, sold at the second exhibition. "I enjoyed the bold colours and finding the pastels in my box." KRW

57

Newspaper coverage reflecting the media frenzy surrounding the second Picturecraft exhibition in July 2010. The 'Mini Monet' tag became famous throughout the world

An amazing array of opportunities presented themselves; an interview with Sir David Frost (Kieron was his youngest interviewee), meeting Philip Schofield and all the Dancing on Ice stars. Kieron also painted alongside Rolf Harris on 3 December that year.

Regardless of everything that Kieron had going on in his spare time, he still maintained good grades at school, and despite not feeling very happy about going to school, Kieron applied himself when he was there. He behaved himself too, and you couldn't possibly ask for anything more.

'Morston Church', watercolour, sold at Kieron's second exhibition.

'Morston to Blakeney, Norfolk', oil, sold at the second exhibition. "I love the muddy puddle in the foreground." KRW

'Pin Mill', oil, sold at the second exhibition. "I spent hours putting the leaves on the trees." KRW

'White Boat' - an oil sold at the second exhibition

'At rest' - an oil sold at the second exhibition

I was then contacted by NBC America who wished to arrange a live broadcast from the gallery over the weekend. It was all rather hectic and quite overwhelming. The satellite van arrived, far too large to negotiate into our Lees Yard site. Fortunately the crew managed to secure a number of car parking spaces on the public car park immediately adjacent to the gallery. As the satellite dish rose automatically above the van, wires were fed through to the gallery where all the filming equipment necessary for a live link to America was being assembled. Kieron was fitted with an earpiece and microphone, taped rather crudely beneath his clothes. Very calmly, he spread out his paints on a side table and commenced painting at my enormous antique studio easel, a treasured artefact retained from my grandfather's days of running the gallery.

As the gallery hushed, Kieron confidently spoke about his love for art and gave a step-by-step account as he progressed with his painting. The family were gathered around him and responded to questions being transmitted from the presenters of the live television show. I whispered to my father to come over to the gallery desk and we watched in silence as hundreds of emails started to appear on the computer screen from America. It was an amazing experience to be standing at the forefront of such instantaneous power being generated by the media... and it quickly became the talk of the town. But this was literally only the start of what was to come. **Adrian Hill**

"I felt the responsibility for Kieron's development one snowy day when only the few had struggled into school and we were outside enjoying the snow. Kieron was eager as ever to join in the snowball fight but couldn't get his gloves on and asked me to help him. I still have nightmares about those talented fingers being attacked by frostbite!" **Beryl Knowles, teacher**

'Winter Walk' - a watercolour sold at Kieron's second exhibition

'Mill at Sunset', pastel

ALL HIS OWN WORK

We are so proud of the fact that Kieron's progress over the last three years is completely down to his own commitment and determination. Picasso had a father who was an art teacher, and other child prodigies often follow in their parent's footsteps. We hear so often that artistic talent runs in families, or is a consequence of the Autism-Asperger's spectrum. We do wonder where Kieron would be, and what work he would be producing if we were more competent or knowledgeable in the field, or if he were surrounded by equally artistic people. But the flip side to that is that Kieron chooses his own subject matter, his own media, his own time and space to paint or draw, without interference, and to us that adds to the beauty of his work, knowing that it is Kieron inspired, not engineered in any other way. We are also very conscious of how limiting we are for Kieron, by not coping particularly well with the pressures that we face; his energy levels seem limitless, and that makes us feel very old at times! But we also remain apprehensive about Kieron experiencing everything now, at such a young age.

We were offered opportunities to exhibit across the globe, and we were thrilled, overwhelmed with the invitations, feeling that Kieron truly deserved to reach the international stage, even at aged eight, and that it seemed a natural progression from the previous local exhibitions. But our health could not withstand the ifs, buts and maybes that we go through as parents with each new scenario. As parents we always want Kieron to have a positive outcome, to sell well, and to receive positive feedback, but to enter such a stage and be open to the scrutiny that can potentially occur, bears too heavy on our shoulders.

Are we wrong for denying Kieron this opportunity? Should it be a decision we override? Or are we right at this moment in time to protect him? If someone has the answers, we'd love to know. What we do know is that the local support we have received is incomparable to the doubts and fears we have of exhibiting abroad, and if it isn't broken, why fix it?

'Marsh at Sunset', pastel, sold at Kieron's third exhibition. "This was the largest pastel I had completed at this time." *KRW*

THE THIRD EXHIBITION

Despite the experience we had under our belts of exhibitions and the media, the third exhibition seemed to take so much more out of us. We were filming and working on the Channel 4 'Child Genius' documentary, which we were enjoying very much. I don't know what it was that drained our energy: that there were people camping outside the gallery two days early devoid of basic home comforts? The feeding frenzy as people ran to take their tickets off the paintings? Or the aftermath and doing four different filming projects in a day? It's only until you go through a process that you realise that you either can't do it again, or that you want to do things very differently the next time. Suddenly every minute of the day and night was spent talking about or dealing with this issue. It became all consuming. Home life was more important than anything else, and we needed to get ourselves back on track.

'Fishing Boats at Cley', a pastel completed live for a Channel 4 TV documentary

Hectic scenes inside Picturecraft Gallery Holt preparing for the NBC broadcast and (right) Adrian Hill being interviewed

Kieron, Keith, Michelle and Billie-Jo had arrived with the documentary camera crew filming for Channel 4. Other international television crews and reporters were also assembled in preparation for the gallery doors to open. The door had been covered to prevent anyone from outside having any awareness where paintings were actually hanging in the gallery. Over the years people have become quite ingenious in finding ways to peep into the gallery before an exhibition opens. As the door was unveiled all we could see were rows of heads and a sound engineer's microphone linked with one of the television film crews. I walked over to Kieron and shook his hand. He looked up at me and grinned. I wished him good luck and then the doors were opened. Customers were literally clawing at the envelopes, ripping them off the paintings in sheer desperation to buy. Telephones were ringing non-stop and all the lines were permanently occupied by my staff who were rushing to quickly remove an envelope when an unsold painting was located. Emails were being received literally by the second and these were opened in order of their timed arrival with staff at the ready to secure a sale whenever possible. Within 30 minutes every painting had been sold! A request was made by one of the television crew for the final envelope to be replaced and then quickly removed once again in order that the moment should be captured on film. With hardly time to take a breath, a television camera was thrust into my face and the interviewer asked the question, "How much? How much has he made?" **Adrian Hill**

If someone would have told me at the beginning of 2010 that I would be flying to England for an art exhibition that summer, I would have thought them mad. But after an extensive online search for artist prodigies yielded just one name – Kieron Williamson – a small group of us decided to make the long journey from various parts of the United States over to Holt, UK. After hopping a flight, train, and finally a taxi, we arrived only to discover that someone had already beat us to the front of the line… 3 days early!

Over the next couple of nights, we bonded, made new friends, and camped out in front of Picturecraft Gallery. When the exhibition opened, each member of our small group was able to purchase a painting and admire all of the other paintings that this young master was able to create. Kieron's work is quite remarkable online and in pictures, but in person, it's even more magnificent. The details and the way that he captures light is truly amazing. Thank you so much to the Williamson's for coming out and meeting us and making the event that much more special for us! **Adam Szewczyk, Arizona, United States**

'Cley Cattle', oil, sold at Kieron's third exhibition. "I painted this on location." KRW

'Cley Sky', oil, sold at Kieron's third exhibition

'Holkham Sunset', pastel, sold at Kieron's third exhibition

'Ducks on the Marsh', pastel, sold at Kieron's third exhibition

'Cromer Waves', pastel, sold at Kieron's third exhibition

'Cley Catch', pastel, sold at Kieron's third exhibition

Above: 'Morston Buoys', pastel, sold at Kieron's third exhibition

Right: 'Cattle Grazing', oil, sold at Kieron's third exhibition. "I love the light in this." KRW

Opposite page: 'Sailing on the Broads', oil, sold at Kieron's third exhibition. "The light catching the sail is a refreshing contrast." KRW

I can distinctly recall the sheer delight on the faces of those queuing when Kieron arrived into Lees Yard that evening with his parents and sister, Billie-Jo. They felt that they had to come in order to express their appreciation and absolute amazement, and found themselves engaged in conversation with all those assembled on the gallery doorstep. The reaction was immediate and an unforgettable experience for all concerned. One guest from America pulled me to one side and said, "What a lovely little boy... such a happy guy!", perfectly describing Kieron's happy-go-lucky attitude and energetic life.

The media attention and international recognition was now making it absolutely impossible for many to compete with art collectors around the world. Kieron's accomplished paintings were now considered quite unique and highly desirable. For a child to receive worldwide recognition for painting remains unrivalled to this day, and is further endorsed through his tremendous ability to use the three painting mediums of oil, pastel and watercolour.

Maybe, one day, what had been accomplished on that particular morning might be recorded somewhere in the history of British painting, and amongst all this sensational interaction, one incredible little boy just sat calmly to one side of the gallery with his mother, father and sister. Occasionally, Kieron was approached by a customer seeking his autograph on one of his greetings card. Most gushingly enthused over his paintings and were so excited that he should know which picture they had been so fortunate to secure. The biggest impression for Kieron however, was when he was told just how much they loved his paintings, and then you would see him beam from ear to ear.

The most important thing for me to treasure from that day was the moment that I was to subsequently share with Kieron and Keith immediately after all the chaos had started to settle down. Kieron asked, "Can we go and play football now?" It seems almost impossible to imagine now, but the three of us sneaked away and I suddenly found myself in a suit and tie kicking a ball around in the play park nearby. It seemed so bizarre that moments before we were selling Kieron's paintings all over the world, and now we were laughing and having so much fun as this 'little artist' scored goal after goal, running rings around me and his father. It just seemed to put everything into perspective. Yes! In the deeply serious world of art, Kieron is a very special, truly amazing, successful little boy. But this day it was equally important to play, and that's exactly what we did, with not a care in the world. **Adrian Hill**

Thankfully Kieron has very different recollections of the exhibition processes, and we have to be careful that we don't assume that he feels the same way. Equally, it was important for Kieron to know how we were feeling too. Kieron looks back on the exhibition with pride and enthusiasm, when I looked over and saw him enveloped in a swarm of people asking for cards to be signed, I wanted to pull him away, but Kieron doesn't remember that aspect of the day, he liked the attention. The visitors from America made the event a magical experience, not only did they take away the fear that nobody would turn up, but despite living outside the gallery for two nights on deck chairs, they remained excited and happy to have met Kieron. We keep in contact, and it is so very humbling to know that people have been touched by Kieron's work to such an extent, that they are prepared to travel half way around the world to buy a painting completed by a seven year old. Their actions were to spur others on to join in the camping!

'Salthouse Street', watercolour, sold at Kieron's third exhibition

'Waiting for FIFA', watercolour, sold at Kieron's third exhibition. "I was waiting for a football match to start and I just had to do something." KRW

'Winter Lakeside', pastel, sold at Kieron's third exhibition. "I enjoy being able to put a variety of colours in the sky." KRW

'Red Coat. Holkham, Norfolk', pastel, sold at Kieron's third exhibition

'Two Trees', oil, sold at Kieron's third exhibition

'Cley Surf', pastel, sold at Kieron's third exhibition

'Mackerel Sky', pastel, sold at Kieron's third exhibition. "The horizon seems a millions miles away in this picture." KRW

'Rustic Reeds', watercolour, sold at Kieron's third exhibition

'Unloading the Catch', watercolour, sold at
Kieron's third exhibition

'Norwich Cathedral', oil, sold at Kieron's third exhibition. "I was so pleased with the sky in this picture." KRW

'Straw Bales', pastel. A Tony Garner art class picture sold at Kieron's third exhibition. "I love the crows flying low to the ground." KRW

'Low Tide, Morston, Norfolk', pastel, sold at Kieron's third exhibition. "I like the simplicity of this scene." KRW

'Norfolk Landscape', oil, painted for NBC TV 2011

'Mount Fuji', oil, painted for Japanese TV 2011

St Benet's Abbey, voted Kieron's favourite painting 2010. "Edward Seago painted it many times and it is believed his ashes were scattered there. Lots of other artists have painted it too." KRW

WHAT MAKES A CHILD GIFTED?

Kieron had his IQ tested by Dr Joan Freeman, Child Psychologist, as part of the 'Child Genius' documentary. It was higher than we expected given Keith's and my educational background and we were so pleased with the result, achieving a place in the top 8 per cent. During an interview with Joan by CNN, Joan describes the elements that enable the development of a gifted child as being love, support and encouragement, opportunity and access. But to us, it's more than that. Billie is exposed to the same love, support, equipment, the same space, in fact Billie has the influence of an artistic older sibling, but she chooses very much to follow her own path. She hopes one day to be famous, but doesn't wish to follow in Kieron's footsteps. She doesn't actively fight against it, nor expressing her dislike at all, but I do believe that Kieron's circumstances came about because of the real intention and focus that he had at that time. And the opportunity to share it on a global level presented itself at that time. Kieron knows that he wants to sell his work, he wants his work to hang in museums, and he wants the Queen to have a collection. He doesn't see age as a barrier in any way.

Billie does not have that same drive and determination. She also produces beautiful work, and is naturally artistic. But would we say that Billie is gifted and talented? Yes, because as parents we believe every child is, unique and special in their own way with their unique merits. Would we claim that her work is better or more advanced than her peers? We would not. Do we offer our praise and celebration of her achievements in the same way we offer to Kieron? Yes we do. Would we encourage her to stand in the public eye for her achievements? We would not, because it is not her wish, or her intention. We didn't go looking for global attention for Kieron either, but we did seek local interest. So to balance the love and encouragement and the time, attention and opportunities between two or more siblings is hard, as any parent knows, but to do so when one child is clearly streets ahead of anybody's game, and one child happy where she is in time, and for us to feel as parents that we have done our best for them both is a curse that I do not wish upon anybody. Having said that, before the media and commercial element arrived in our laps, we treated the children equally with encouragement and enthusiasm, money was tight to lavish them with material goods, so we did what we could with those things that we feel are of value: unconditional love and friendship. What would we do if the same circumstances arose for Billie? Don't ask!

We don't use the term 'prodigy' often, or fully appreciate the meaning of the word really, but if we were asked is Kieron gifted and talented, then we would say yes, without doubt. Our main aim however, is to keep grounded and maintain a normal routine, for Kieron to be accepted by his peers and not isolated. Kieron is multifaceted, he's so much more than his artwork, and so for us to create an imbalance by pushing him down a particular route would be detrimental to his well-being and bring more stress. It's our job at this moment in time to ensure that he keeps up with his schoolwork and his other interests.

For more information: www.joanfreeman.co.uk/talent.htm

'St Benet's Abbey', pastel. "This is my favourite place to paint." KRW

DILEMMAS

We are so conscious of the revenue potential as pointed out to us by various parties, that as parents we have an inbuilt aversion to that. We are however constantly badgered by Kieron to continue to with the sales of his work. Kieron's unique and innocent brand and identity are important to us, and it has led to many disappointing decisions to decline the help and support of larger companies and galleries in order to keep Kieron's brand as it is. What Kieron chooses to do with it when he is old enough to take over is up to him; we do not want to enter into a situation now that he may regret when he's older.

The question of exploitation arose at a painting demonstration Kieron offered to raise funds for the Swaffham Rotary Club, in Oct 2010. A lady from the audience had asked. As parents, we knew that we were following the guidance and instruction of our then, eight year old son. The funds raised from the sale of Kieron's art, minus the cost of materials, go straight to Kieron. The intentions of other people who wish to become associated with Kieron will have to judge for themselves and prepare to be judged, and we do not doubt for one moment the integrity of our decisions to date.

As parents we do not look at Kieron's situation through commercial eyes. And we remain at this moment in time lucky to have a stream of interest so that we don't need to advertise or enter into a marketing strategy. We don't know if we are making the right move, or the right decisions, for now it seems to meet Kieron's wishes, settling the children into a new school and environment will bring its own challenges, so far the support that we have offered the children and each other has had good results, so we have to trust our judgement and carry on as we are.

Family photo taken by Adam Szewczyk during his visit from Arizona

Kieron under the camera's eye

The family during the filming of Kieron painting the picture for the Swaffham Rotary Club

'Broadland Lookout', watercolour, painted 'live' for Dutch, French and Russian TV, November 2011

THE GREAT KIERON PHENOMENON

Our life before fame was simple and poor, but so rewarding. We wanted that back. We were suddenly living in a flat that had shrunk overnight, we felt claustrophobic, and despite the enthusiasm that still surrounded us, it wasn't enough to tempt us to continue. The Kieron phenomenon had become too big for us to grow into comfortably, I kept asking for us to have baby steps, so that we could cope and catch up in our own time, but it was frustrating to those around us. Media events and future sales and exhibitions were all cancelled in a frantic attempt to survive.

We went into meltdown, thankfully. For someone who hits burnout regularly, it was a welcome relief, time to recoup and recover. Health suffered, Keith had blood pressure fears and for me, depression and the phobic anxiety returned. I had left my job as a practitioner and went into hibernation, unable to answer the telephone at times. Even daily routines were hard work. The Kieron Phenomenon was just too big to live with. We approached Kieron and asked if he minded if we stopped selling his work, he was devastated. This wasn't the first time we had asked him! We compromised on a break, to take a year off, and to prioritise a house move.

Was the impact worse on us because of the speed of events, or that it was unexpected, or because the fame found us, rather than us searching for it? If you plan for something does it make it more manageable? If you are in control and making your own decisions are things easier to discuss, rationalise, justify? The fact that we didn't feel in control I think was the crux of the matter, it was going too fast for us to breathe, and we didn't recognise anything anymore. At the same time, we were faced with disappointing our son, failing him, unable to shelve the stress and just enjoy the magical gift he was sharing. We couldn't see things from his perspective and he couldn't see things from our perspective. The emotional roller coaster was a daily event for us.

Kieron painting on glass 'live' for a Submarine Films series of short documentaries, May 2011

Part of the emotional roller coaster: Michelle, Kieron and Keith at a live broadcast from the Picturecraft gallery, July 2010

Adrian Hill and Kieron at the printer with one of Kieron's limited edition prints

I was now to find myself challenged in another direction. Inevitably, those who had purchased some of Kieron's earlier work suddenly recognised the value of the painting now hanging on their wall. The question of resale began to surface where clients wished to capitalise on the current market values for their paintings, and others became concerned that they needed to assess a valuation for insurance purposes. I was faced with the moral issue of customers now wishing me to become actively involved in cases where the love of the painting had completely disappeared, to be replaced with the concept of 'let's make a quick sale whilst the going is good'. I was distressed with the situation, but reluctantly had to accept the argument that customers were entitled to commercial opportunities during times of extremely high demand. I felt it was far better for me to be in control of the situation rather than standing by and letting others find random initiatives to dispose of Kieron's work. At the very least it would enable us to be in a position to monitor the movements of paintings and have a greater knowledge of the outcome. I have been in the art trade long enough to know that some clients had made speculative early purchases of Kieron's artwork purely to invest. Whereas this is a relatively common practice in the world of art, in this particular instance the unprecedented international attention for Kieron's paintings had inflated the average price of a painting by 600 per cent in less than six months. Where the adult world has a daily understanding of financial speculation, the unimaginable effect this had through the eyes of a seven year old boy was very dramatic. Kieron's perception on the whole issue was painfully simplistic and he questioned the reasoning for his work being resold, 'Why are the people who told me that they loved my work suddenly deciding that they don't want it anymore?'

The power of the internet enabled access for literally millions of people to discover the world of Kieron Williamson. But this inquisitive little boy was equally able to type his own name into a search engine to discover what was happening to his own paintings. He was shattered to discover that a gift of a painting to an assistant at his primary school was being displayed for sale on one of the most powerful online auction sites in the world. His reaction to this sudden realisation of betrayal almost stopped Kieron from picking up a paint brush again. But this was only just the first instance. With around 150 paintings released to date, there have been a few instances of resale paintings. Not surprisingly, the vast majority of my customers retain their treasured original Kieron Williamson painting with great affection, genuinely overjoyed to have been in a position to assist this young man along his artistic journey.

I reflected on the all the positives and negatives that had arisen throughout the year. I recognised that both Keith and Michelle were struggling to come to terms with the issue of paintings being re-sold. The continual dilemma of pricing paintings had always been a concern and finding ways to placate the overwhelming pressure from every aspect of the media had placed additional pressures on us all. I had been made acutely aware that there had been times when Kieron's brushes had been packed away, paintings had been torn in half, and mention made that 'I'm not going to paint any more'. I was to receive text messages on my mobile telephone, many of which I have kept to remind me of how fragile situations could become. There were times when I found myself deeply regretting the opportunities when the world of business clouded pleasurable moments which could have easily compromised our friendship.
Adrian Hill

RUNNING AWAY?

During another week in Cornwall, in October 2010, life in the South West was even more appealing, with fresh sea air, coastal walks of breath-taking beauty, and sunrise at Polperro. We couldn't wait. But we were also looking to run away. From what, we can't express, but we decided to work towards a resolution, keeping the sales element intact somehow at Kieron's insistence, but to find a way so that we could cope. Cornwall offered us all something, and perhaps we could continue with the commercial element to Kieron's painting if we had a change of scenery.

When our holiday to Cornwall came to a close, Kieron was devastated, we saw him standing at the edge of the Looe Estuary, shoulders dropped, lip dropped, toes nudging at the mud, tears in his eyes, we were determined to move down there. After spending December and early January looking and planning, a few offers on various properties including one in a flood zone sadly scared us sufficiently to look closer to home.

A chance Norfolk property search revealed that a beautiful cottage had been reduced. A Friday of enquiries and a Saturday of viewing led to an offer being accepted. We were thrilled, and didn't mind much that it wasn't Cornwall. It would offer the children a bedroom each, Kieron some studio space other than having to share the kitchen table and has the potential for business use to run our own gallery. It ticked all the boxes, apart from not being on the Cornish coast, but it would give Kieron a sound investment and a home for the future.

The following months would see the children settle at their new school, gain in confidence and Keith and I feeling better than we had in long time. But Cornwall was still tugging at our heart strings.

CORNWALL 2010

Kieron on the rocks

Kieron and Billie-Jo on the beach

Kieron and Grandad

Kieron feeling the loss of having to leave Cornwall, October 2010

'Daphne Du Maurier's former home, Bodinnick, Cornwall', watercolour

It has been a privilege to play a part, albeit a small one, in Kieron's early life and I watch his growth with interest... and yes, Kieron, I would love to see your pictures for many years to come. **Beryl Knowles, teacher**

As the Williamson's were preparing for a long overdue holiday, a return visit to their beloved Cornwall, talks of moving down South became quite serious. I was frequently asked what I thought about them moving away from Norfolk. My genuine response was, and will always remain the same, 'As long as they are happy, that's all that is important'. This however was certainly not what people wished me to say. There was a real passion, particularly from my local customers, that Kieron was a Norfolk boy. A very real sense of disquiet was being felt that it would be such a shame for them to move away. I knew that if Kieron was happy he would paint. It really wouldn't matter whether he was in Cornwall, Norfolk, or anywhere else.

October 2010 arrived and the release of Channel 4 Television's 'Child Genius' programme generated another enormous wave of media attention. The documentary was extremely interesting, showcasing some very gifted children with exceptionally special skills. I was surprised at the high level of parental pressure being placed on the majority of the children featuring in the documentary. There also seemed to be a distinct lack of creativity for most of the children. Learning to play a piano in order to become an accomplished pianist demanded high levels of one-to-one tuition. Similarly, a child studying chess revealed monotonous hours of teaching in order to learn the moves to play.

Kieron contrasted so sharply to the rigid educational structures associated with learning. He was most eloquent in his delivery and quick to point out that he was reliant on nobody for guidance or instruction. He was completely self-taught and proved that he could start a painting from scratch and finish with a most accomplished work of art. This creative 'child genius' from Norfolk was revealed to be a most happy, well-adjusted, normal little boy with a beautiful smile and wonderful sense of mischief. Sequences were shown that included him painting and playing football, but for me the closing credits of the programme revealed Kieron at his best. He was seen pedalling furiously as fast as he could on his bicycle in a race to try and beat the cameraman filming from a car by his side!

An aspect of the documentary involved a critique on Kieron's artwork from two extremely knowledgeable specialists in fine art. One of London's top gallery owners and an art historian were interviewed to establish their personal opinions, and each gave tremendous amounts of merit and encouragement stating, 'It's what he will do next that is so important'.

Keith and Michelle were justifiably proud that Kieron shone through in the documentary amongst some of the most gifted children of his age group in the UK.

Whilst immensely busy, I experienced the feeling of something missing in my day-to-day routine. Each day never passed without opportunities arising to engage with customers and visitors enquiring about Kieron, his incredible paintings, his television appearances and his extraordinary success. **Adrian Hill.**

THE FOURTH EXHIBITION

We couldn't go through 2011 without a request for an exhibition, and we couldn't turn down an opportunity for Kieron to exhibit in Devon. It was reassuring to know that Keith and I could organise an event on our own, in between decorating and moving house. Delamore House did a fantastic job of coping with global enquiries and achieving another sell-out exhibition, and sadly without us being able to attend. The media interviews promoting the event led to a premature leak of our new location and the village knew of our arrival before the school did. Anonymity had failed. The exhibition however was a great opportunity to show Kieron's appreciation of the landscapes of the South West of England as well as Norfolk favourites.

'Misty Morning,' sold at the 2011 Delamore Arts Exhibition in Devon

'Boats at Bodinnick, Fowey,' watercolour, exhibited at Delamore 2011. "Cornwall is special because of the huge height of the coastal and estuary edges, with dense foliage." KRW

'Morning Shift, Looe, Cornwall', watercolour, exhibited at Delamore 2011.

'Low Tide - Kingsbridge, Devon', watercolour, exhibited at Delamore 2011.

'Polperro Harbour', watercolour, exhibited at Delamore 2011.

'Boats moored at Fowey, Cornwall', watercolour

INVESTING FOR THE FUTURE

Having come from a position where money was tight and not really a problem because there was never any surplus; when the situation arose with Kieron's new found wealth, we panicked. We sought immediate help to make sure that there was a visible paper trail, we were so acutely aware of people's perceptions and scrutiny, that we wanted it to be kept as safe and as separate from our finances as we could. Where do you put savings in the current financial climate? Kieron had chosen to buy a big chest of Sennelier pastels; the wooden chest resembles a coffee table! Kieron has also chosen to buy his own Seago paintings, and other works that have influenced his art and fuelled his passion. I remember Kieron sitting at the table happily announcing one evening 'I've got tax'. I think it gave him a sense of being on par with other adults, always in such a hurry to be a grown up, in fact if he could drive a car tomorrow he wouldn't hesitate at all.

Property investment became an option. We were somewhat naïve in expecting the process to be an easy one, and that the available cash would be sufficient. But the eyes of the law have different views on competence below the age of eighteen and this deepened the ethical minefield we found ourselves in. Thankfully the fame and fortune has not turned Kieron into an arrogant ass, he remains just as he was, grateful that people like his work and they want to buy it because they like it. We have been extremely lucky to have the support of a great accountant, bookkeeper and legal team that have helped orientate us through this process, keeping everything in Trust until Kieron reaches eighteen.

The family share in the pleasure of Kieron's success at a Picturecraft exhibition

'Winter at Thornage, Norfolk', pastel, sold at Kieron's fifth exhibition

PAINTING PROGRESS

We are asked numerous times where does Kieron get his talent, I'd like to think it was me, in fact one cold and recent January afternoon, Kieron announced 'mum, you must have more talent than me, because you gave birth to me and I have this talent just in art, so you must have more talent' well that confirmed it, straight from the horse's mouth!

I loved art at school, and spent hours upstairs in my room drawing. But I didn't really produce anything especially good. Keith can draw too if he has to, but again it is restrained and what you would expect. Billie was more naturally drawn to pens and pencils at a young age, inspired by the craft activities at pre-school, and can create anything out of the recycling bin, a recent project was to turn some card shoe moulds into pixie boots!!

It's the speed at which Kieron progresses that amazes us, every three months or so he goes up another level. Why does a young boy choose to go out and paint on location in the freezing cold, Salthouse marshes, Cley sluice, it's during those time you completely forget he's a child. Kieron is extremely self-motivated and always looking at the skies, the tree line, the wild life and seasonal changes. He's also got the World Wide Web at his fingertips, which has led to a curiosity of other artists, other countries and cultures and a greater appreciation of architectural differences and complexities. It also exposes Kieron to an even wider array of styles and techniques.

Cows used to feature just on the horizon as indistinct blobs, but as Kieron gained in confidence, he would draw them slightly bigger and they would then feature in the mid ground and now in the foreground of his work. Suggestions of figures became more prominent in his work until he reached a stage where he felt confident to try portraits.

Kieron began with watercolours, acrylics and brush pens, and soon progressed onto oils, not liking their fluidity or lengthy drying time. He also didn't like the faster drying oils, but persevered and grew to love oils, pastels and watercolours equally. We are pleased that he has kept his hand in with all three, and despite having 'popular sellers' Kieron is not tempted to become too commercial and repaint scenes because of this.

It was difficult at times to keep up with him. Kieron would produce a watercolour painting before we got out of bed, then he'd move onto oils, expect you to clear up and wash out his brushes before he went on to do a pastel, a weekend could produce 4-5 paintings. Sharing the kitchen table had been hard for Kieron, to have to stop at meal times. I used to cuss as I stubbed my toe on his easel, but I was told I should feel blessed!! So the cussing had to stop and I grew to accept that the kitchen table and floor were to be wiped before a meal, after a meal, after an oil, after a pastel or two and after a watercolour. We would eat from our laps frequently, as the table waited for Kieron to return. Surfaces and radiators became drying spaces, shelves and kitchen drawers were taken over by art equipment, the atmosphere took on a whole new dimension, a vitality and energy that raised us all to a different level, and we missed it hugely whenever it waned.

After our last trip to Cornwall, Kieron chose not to paint for a month or two. This wasn't a surprise really; it was almost as if Norfolk didn't hold the same inspiration for him anymore. For a while we almost reached normal again, we were fine with Kieron's choice, looking at the bigger picture and thinking that one day, inspiration would smack him between the eyes and he might want to capture it again on paper.

Kieron is equally at home painting outdoors...

...or in the studio

'Barge at Blakeney', a favourite early watercolour

Would we be disappointed if he gave it up? We would enjoy the peace and quiet, the privacy and normal family activities, but the artwork has been a best friend to Kieron, it has improved his communication skills, his confidence, and his self-expression. It has kept him out of trouble, stopped him from being bored, improved his concentration at school, and widened his areas of interest and his keen attention to detail.

Kieron's love of nature, his surroundings and the landscape is quite deep for a young lad of nine. He'll hear the geese fly overhead before we do and will stop and watch their changing formations. We were so lucky in the flat to be able to see the sunrise out of one window and watch it set out of another. We were always taking photos, even locally, walking around like a couple of tourists!! Keith and Kieron enjoyed a Sunday walk to Letheringsett, or to Glandford. Kieron was a sponge for information on birds and wildlife, enjoying 'Countryfile', David Attenborough, 'Deadliest Catch', etc.

If Kieron were to hang up his paintbrushes, he would spend his time mastering some other activity, maybe football, maybe something else, but Kieron's personality is such, that he will give 200 per cent, and I imagine that he'll want to be the best or be world famous for whatever he does!! Where does he get that? As a toddler, Kieron declared that he was going to be world famous...

A session with Rolf Harris in December 2010 saw the return of some interest, and when we revisited Ludham, Kieron felt fully inspired to paint again. Like a best friend had called round and asked him to play, it was Edward Seago's work that had brought Kieron back to his brushes. Winter has been a key element in Kieron's works. You can feel the coldness leaching out from the paper stinging your nose, the signature strategically placed in the mud, the icy water or the snow, exactly where Kieron would choose to be standing if he could climb into the canvas. Some close friends see this connection with Seago and Kieron has received many books on Seago as gifts.

'Bluebell Walk' pastel

'Lone Boat', oil, in the style of Monet

*'Jack's Sky', oil, painted in memory of
the Norfolk artist Jack Cox*

Opposite page: 'Poppies at Hunworth', oil

'Salthouse Haze', oil

'Scarecrow' oil

'Poppies at Letheringsett' pastel

Kieron in his studio at Ludham

To ignore the influence that Keith's job has on Kieron would be wrong. Keith had to put his hobby into practice and find a viable means of income after being deemed unsafe on a stepladder. A common misconception is that as an art dealer Kieron has been encouraged down this route because of the revenue potential. But we had witnessed the plight of other artists struggling to make ends meet and we certainly wouldn't be encouraging Kieron to be putting all his eggs in one basket at this age, just as we refuse to put all our eggs into his basket, despite his popularity and recent sell-outs. Kieron's art is a hobby, a very lucrative one, but just that. Life goes on and school remains a priority. The art world can be such a fickle one also, and putting your child out there to be scrutinised by the world is the toughest thing for us to do. Unlike abstract art that can pass quite easily before people's eyes, either to be accepted or quite simply not, as in the case of Marmite, Kieron's style and intent on capturing the world as he appreciates it is heavily scrutinised, able to be critiqued against clearly measurable criterion. Many critics, all-willing to share with us their opinions, have approached us. But, Kieron's work has progressed beyond our wildest expectations in such a short space of time and in three different medium, gradually the naive elements of his work dropping off like flies as his attention to detail and understanding of the world of nature, architecture and construction becomes ever clearer to him. We were astonished by the recent critique by Jonathan Jones, Guardian, Nov 2011, who acknowledges Kieron's presence amongst the world's other great artists we've loved and admired.

Keith is a channel in which Kieron can see and learn about the vast number of artists and paintings that pass through auction. This enables Kieron to see old and new, listed and unlisted. It's like seeing an Argos catalogue just before Christmas!! The qualities that Keith has are consistency and loyalty to his interests; I think Kieron has these too. Despite Kieron's interest in cars, trains and dinosaurs coming and going when he was younger, his interest in, and loyalty towards art has remained. They share a passion for Leeds United too!! Quite spiritual in a football kind of way.

So many artists have told us that anyone can paint, but not everyone can draw, they would insist that Kieron draw and draw to the point of frustration then to draw again. We didn't see any conscious effort from Kieron to draw for the sake of it until year 3 at school, when simple sketches would arrive home in his bookbag. We were delighted to see this, and with no encouragement needed, Kieron has progressed to such a level that he amazed us even more. He continued however to perform the classic Kieron traits, drawing a beautiful scene on a canvas board, leave it kicking around for a week or two, then rub it out when he changed his mind on the purpose of the board. Or he would produce a beautiful drawing and later produce a beautiful watercolour, directly on the reverse of the paper!! We would love for Kieron to work through a sketch pad from left to right, complete it before moving onto another, so that numbering, logging and storing the work was easy, but he doesn't, so we do our best to work around it.

Kieron was invited by Submarine Films, A Dutch Film crew to paint on location on a sheet of glass. They wanted to edit a short film, witnessing Kieron disappearing into a landscape. It was a great privilege to do this project with a producer that focused on the painting itself, rather than the sales aspect. Kieron loved the attention and the project and despite high winds and some apprehension as to the proximity to the water's edge, it was a great result. The framed piece hangs in Kieron's studio.

WHY LANDSCAPES AND NATURE?

Kieron has been informally exposed to many various styles of art through galleries, googling artists, looking through magazines and auction catalogues etc, absorbing contemporary art, abstract, collage and sculpture, but he still chooses to paint scenes that can be recognised. It's interesting to see a young boy admire the beauty in cold damp days, Kieron's commitment to working on location in the freezing cold and Keith's commitment to be there, holding the palette is remarkable. Kieron used to paint the same scene from a photograph time and time again, but it wasn't until he painted on site, that we could see the difference it made to his work, there was movement in the skies, the shadows tracing across the landscape after the sunshine. One day an otter chose to splash around in the water right in front of them, they stood watching it play for over five minutes before remembering they had two cameras!! That made the painting so much more significant and we began to keep more paintings back from sale.

Kieron will admit that walking the same streets as Seago did, looking at the same trees that were around when Munnings, Cotman and Seago were alive, is spine tingling, and adds to the inspiration. Seeing the cliffs disappear at Trimingham, is inconceivable to Kieron, a crime, theft by mother nature and serious neglect. What could be better than running through a stubble field with the spray from the sea in your face? Kieron's loyalty to landscape painting is evident, despite the occasional portrait, cityscape, horse study etc., he returns to landscapes easily and soulfully.

'Barn Owl' an early painting

Painting from nature

'Cornish Cream, Mevagissey', oil. Kieron's largest painting to date was shown at the fifth exhibition. It was acquired by the Reich Insurance Group and now hangs in their board room.

THE FIFTH EXHIBITION

November 2011 saw a return to the familiarity and warmth of Holt and the Picturecraft Gallery, and another sell-out exhibition. With film crews from Denmark, France, Germany and Russia alongside local crews, it was a great event. The burning desire to run away to Cornwall was less this time and walking across the marshes before and after filming events helped to reduce the impact of stress on our health, it seems we have found a balance. To be contemplating another exhibition in 2012 already means we must be coping at least.

'Brancaster Sunset', watercolour

This time I was able to work well ahead of the exhibition with many of the media contacts who had expressed an interest in covering the event. An exceptionally busy time was forecast with regional television crews and six international television film crews pledging their desire to attend the preview opening. For the first time a Norwegian documentary crew registered interest.

Despite freezing conditions, the first two clients arrived the night before the exhibition and bravely camped outside on the gallery doorstep. At 4am they were joined by a gentleman who had journeyed from Taiwan in order to hopefully secure one of Kieron's paintings. As media and customers arrived in preparation of the doors opening at 9am, I announced that, due to the small number of paintings being exhibited, it would only be possible for one customer to purchase one painting. This was accepted without question. **Adrian Hill**

'St Benet's Abbey', watercolour, sold at the fifth exhibition

'The Wellington Arch, Hyde Park, London', watercolour, sold at the fifth exhibition

'Frosty Reeds at Thornage', pastel, sold at the fifth exhibition

'Broadland Mist', oil, sold at the fifth exhibition

'Tacking Home', oil, sold at the fifth exhibition

'Cool Shade', pastel, sold at the fifth exhibition

'St Benet's Sunset', pastel, sold at the fifth exhibition. "It was nice to achieve a great contrast in such a small space." KRW

SECRETS TO KIERON'S SUCCESS

Isometimes wonder if the need to overcompensate for my perceived shortcomings had influenced how I behaved towards Kieron. I do know that the British are quite reserved in showing enthusiasm, and having done a parenting course fairly early on, I realised that the normal reaction to misbehaviour is very often a negative one. Thank goodness for TV programmes like Super Nanny, Kieron and I would watch this together and his insight into the different issues astounded me. Children soon know when they are doing the wrong thing, but do they know when they are doing things right, or brilliant, or truly breath-taking? How easy is it to celebrate what is 'right, brilliant or amazing' in a given situation, or to give children options, and maybe a get out clause when there is trouble or dispute? Why does the grown up have to win? Why does there have to be a pecking order?

What works for us is unconditional positive regard, give or take the odd day when PMT is all consuming! Generally, life is easier to live and enjoy if everyone is a winner at something. How busy parents are during times of creativity can make or break a window of opportunity, and I think Joan Freeman hits the nail on the head. It's not about providing a wealth of equipment, or endless experiences but the value in what is provided and the genuine interest that you show. I am so proud of the fact that we have all achieved something great, in a two bed roomed flat, with no garden, with regular schooling, and an abundance of good humour and tolerance.

Kieron's success however, is all credit to Kieron, we may have provided the initial enthusiasm and encouragement, but it is down to Kieron's persistence and determination that has fuelled his passion. It was so out of character, and so unexpected, but so too was Kieron's concentration at school, his ability to apply himself and retain good grades. If he is not sitting at 'the top of the tree', he's not happy. His persistence in breaking learning barriers is phenomenal. He shows limitless determination on the sports field where giving 200 per cent is a regular occurrence. Kieron once ran the 400 meters with a full bladder; he was desperate not to miss the race, and won, albeit with tears in his eyes! Despite Kieron's abilities, the confidence doesn't always match those achievements; he's a sensitive soul and requires at times very sensitive handling.

Kieron is different with his art. It's his chill out time, his hobby, and his evening companion. He can't just sit and do nothing; he's got to be doing something. He relaxes and de-stresses whilst he's drawing. The atmosphere in the house when Kieron is at his table top easel or crouched in front of the TV is difficult to describe, but it is a wonderful thing, he's in the zone, and we enjoy the break from the football crashing down the hallway, ricocheting off the radiators and banister!! What a gift, for someone so young to find a niche like that, an activity, and a hobby that not only makes them feel settled, but one that brings so much to others as well. We all get something out of Kieron's artwork. When he creates a new picture, it can take me a week or two before I can digest the fact that it has come from Kieron. It's so hard for us to accept that the work has come from a nine year old, and we've watched him doing it!! Naively I thought that I would know and understand my children, especially being so close to them, but I really don't understand them. Other people, who spend every waking minute thanking their lucky stars for all that they have in the world, will know what I spend my days doing too.

Keith and I had to make a conscious decision to run with this opportunity, it was a very quick decision, and had we thought everything through, I don't know if we would have made the same

Kieron, Michelle and Billie-Jo

'Sunrise at Morston', oil. "This was my biggest oil to date and we had to stick it down on the table so I could reach the corners. I'm amazed the horizon is straight!" KRW

choices. We never imagined that the hype would continue, just as we never imagined Kieron would stick at something for longer than a few months. He proved us wrong, and the world proved us wrong. Interest in Kieron's work is so great that newspapers and news channels contact us regularly for the latest news.

If this book has any sort of message, or purpose other than illustrating the bizarre chronological run of events, hopefully it shows that the greatest things are right under our noses; we just need to be open to see them. Children get such bad press, and I hope and pray that mine will stay grounded and good, quite what the future holds, nobody knows, but I just hope that Kieron's interest in his art continues to spark the imagination in other children, we receive so many emails from people 'who don't usually email strangers' but for some reason have felt the need to write and thank Kieron for giving them the encouragement to pick up their paint brushes again, and pursue their dreams.

We live in a world where opinions are free, and freely shared, irrespective of the impact they have on another person's feelings, we are at the mercy of the world's attention, and living life in the spot light is a massive responsibility, so too is the huge responsibility that has been placed on Kieron's young shoulders, to be compared to Picasso, Monet and other great artists is overwhelming. We don't know if Kieron will continue to paint or not, London galleries are now willing to invest in the possibility of Kieron being one of those great artists, but it is still a gamble for most. Some galleries would rather wait until Kieron has become slightly more polished, or established, while others see the revenue potential already and wish to reap the rewards now.

THE SIXTH EXHIBITION

Another kind invitation was extended to include work from Kieron at the 2012 Delamore Arts Annual Exhibition of Painting and Sculpture in support of the RNLI. The exhibition, celebrating its tenth year in 2012, is Devon's largest annually run art and sculpture exhibition, held in the impressive Delamore house and gardens situated in Cornwood. Two of the principal rooms in the house are used as galleries for hanging the paintings. Immense windows provide excellent natural light and visitors have an opportunity to view the paintings at leisure within this impressive country house. The gardens too provide a superb showcase for the sculpture and in this setting visitors can view the works of leading artists set against the background of impressive parkland trees and well-tended flowerbeds. The sale of Kieron's work has contributed greatly to the various charities supported.

Delamore, Devon. Home to the county's largest annual art and sculpture exhibition.

'Fowey Mist', oil on box canvas, shown at the tenth annual exhibition at Delamore in 2012.

'Cley Mill from the Marshes', oil. Exhibited at the seventh exhibition

THE SEVENTH EXHIBITION

To conclude things as they stand is impossible, Kieron continues living his dream and we are unable to dampen the spirit within him that finds its way on to canvas and paper. As parents, we would welcome the end of commercial sales, for it has been the most difficult experience we have ever faced. Our ethical debate and emotional roller coaster is with us daily, but we remain touched and encouraged by the constant stream of new emails thanking us for sharing Kieron's gift and for inspiring so many people. We have discovered many new friends along the way, and relationships with existing friends have deepened as we have been supported throughout this remarkable journey. We are so thankful that ultimately we have two happy, expressive and multi-faceted children that amaze us on a daily basis.

The decision to hold a retrospective solo exhibition at age nine was important for us, to round off Kieron's youth-art with a celebration. 2012 is a year of many significant events including the Olympics, the Queens Diamond Jubilee, Kieron reaching ten years of age, and the Picturecraft Gallery also celebrates some significant anniversaries too.

With articles describing Kieron within the same context as other great East Anglian artists, and the art critique by Jonathan Jones in the *Guardian* in November 2011, Kieron's work is no longer seen as being produced by a child, nor is his work compared to the work of other children. The retrospective solo exhibition accompanies this book in celebrating this astonishing accomplishment.

May 2008 saw a shift in Kieron's consciousness and a desire to be a landscape artist. Within four years Kieron has achieved works of a standard that many artists strive to achieve over a lifetime. What Kieron chooses to do from aged ten onwards remains to be seen and we wait with great anticipation to see what he does over the next four years.

'Loch Garry', watercolour. Exhibited at the seventh exhibition

'Returning Home' a watercolour painting of Eric Edwards, Reedcutter, displayed at Kieron's seventh exhibition

'Thurne Mill in February', oil on board. Exhibited at the seventh exhibition

'Winter Shadows, Staithe Road', oil on board. Exhibited at the seventh exhibition

'Winter Morning', watercolour. Exhibited at the seventh exhibition

'Winter Lane', watercolour. Exhibited at the seventh exhibition

'Cattle Shed, Cold Harbour', watercolour. Exhibited at the seventh exhibition

'Snow at Dusk', oil. Exhibited at the seventh exhibition

'Looe Beach, Cornwall', pastel. Exhibited at the seventh exhibition

'Marsh Harrier Hunting' , pastel. Exhibited at the seventh exhibition

'Sea Breeze', pastel. Exhibited at the seventh exhibition

'A Favourite Spot, Morston', oil. Exhibited at the seventh exhibition

'Polperro Harbour', oil. Exhibited at the seventh exhibition

'Toward Cleopatra's Needle', watercolour. Exhibited at the seventh exhibition

'Cley Mill', watercolour. Exhibited at the seventh exhibition

'Blakeney Blue', pastel. Exhibited at the seventh exhibition

'St Benet's at Sunset', pastel. Exhibited at the seventh exhibition

'Victoria Embankment', oil on board. Exhibited at the seventh exhibition

'Broadland Haze', pastel. Exhibited at the seventh exhibition

'Winterton Sunrise', pastel. Exhibited at the seventh exhibition

'*Autumn Walk*', *pastel. Exhibited at the seventh exhibition*

'Wensum Weir', pastel. *Exhibited at the seventh exhibition*

*'Crisp Day, St Benet's Drainage Mill', watercolour.
Exhibited at the seventh exhibition*

*'Sheep Grazing', watercolour. Exhibited
at the seventh exhibition*